This Notebook Belongs To

www.ingramcontent.com/pod-product-compliance
Lightning Source LLC
LaVergne TN
LVHW081602060526
838201LV00054B/2022